(1974)

£3

ART

/PA.

(5th

FIDELIO
OR
WEDDED LOVE

ENGLISH VERSIONS OF OPERA LIBRETTI

THE ABDUCTION FROM THE SERAGLIO
ABU HASSAN
UN BALLO IN MASCHERA
THE BARBER OF SEVILLE
BEATRICE AND BENEDICK
BENVENUTO CELLINI
DR. MIRACLE
DON GIOVANNI
DON PASQUALE
L'ELISIR D'AMORE
EUGENE ONEGIN
FIDELIO
FRA DIAVOLO
DER FREISCHÜTZ
THE MAGIC FLUTE
THE MARRIAGE OF FIGARO
MARTHA
ORPHEUS
THE QUEEN OF SPADES
RIGOLETTO
LA TRAVIATA
THE TROJANS
IL TROVATORE

FIDELIO

OR

WEDDED LOVE

———

AN OPERA IN TWO ACTS

———

Words adapted from the French of
J. N. BOUILLY
by
J. F. SONNLEITHNER
and
F. TREITSCHKE

English Version by
EDWARD J. DENT

Music by
LUDWIG VAN BEETHOVEN

LONDON
OXFORD UNIVERSITY PRESS
NEW YORK   TORONTO

Oxford University Press, Ely House, London W.1

GLASGOW NEW YORK TORONTO MELBOURNE WELLINGTON
CAPE TOWN IBADAN NAIROBI DAR ES SALAAM LUSAKA ADDIS ABABA
DELHI BOMBAY CALCUTTA MADRAS KARACHI LAHORE DACCA
KUALA LUMPUR SINGAPORE HONG KONG TOKYO

NOTE

Stage, radio, television, motion picture, performing, and all other rights subsisting in this English translation are strictly reserved. Permission to perform the work or any part of it in costume, or the complete work in concert form, must be obtained from the publishers (or their agents abroad) who will quote terms on application. Permission to perform excerpts in concert form must be obtained from the Performing Rights Society (London) or from the Society's representatives for performances outside the United Kingdom.

ISBN 0 19 313302 4

First edition 1938
Ninth impression 1974

PRINTED IN GREAT BRITAIN

PREFACE

WHEN the first of all operas was produced at Florence towards the end of the sixteenth century (the date is uncertain) the book of words was printed (in 1600) probably as a souvenir to be given away to the noble ladies and gentlemen who had been invited to the performance, and ever since then it has been the custom to print the words of operas as a little book—hence the international name for it, *libretto*, a little book. The first librettos were written by real poets; in fact the words were often better than the music. As long as operas were composed mainly for the cultivated classes, librettos maintained a reasonably high standard, in whatever language they were written. Quinault wrote in French for Lully, Dryden for Purcell in the seventeenth century; in Italy Apostolo Zeno and Metastasio carried on the tradition of literary dignity into the eighteenth. That century, too, is the great age of comic opera, with admirable humorists such as Goldoni, Bickerstaffe, Sedaine, and Casti—the Gilbert of his day—to say nothing of Mozart's friend Da Ponte. It was not until the days of Verdi—from about 1840 onwards—that the word *libretto* became a byword for nonsense and doggerel. Verdi's audiences were noisy and ill-educated; they wanted roaring melodrama (the word *melodramma* is the classical Italian word for *opera*, which about 1650 was still rather colloquial), with music that could be taken up for political purposes. No wonder that there are still nice-minded people who say they prefer their operas in a language they do not understand.

Opera in English dates back to 1656, but after the death of Purcell in 1695 it languished. Italian opera was established as a fashionable entertainment, and opera in English was only what we should call 'musical comedy'. Out of this comic opera grew what in the nineteenth century was known as 'grand romantic opera'; and its English landmarks were Weber's *Oberon*, written for London, 1826, and the English performances of Beethoven's *Fidelio* (with Malibran as the heroine) in 1833. But it is difficult to translate bad Italian into anything but worse English, and the result has been that opera in English is to most people a lamentably ridiculous affair. Opera in English will never flourish until a tradition of really good translation is established. Far be it from me to speak ill of my predecessors: Thomas Oliphant's version of *Fidelio* (1833) is a model of good style. Unfortunately it sounds too elegant for the present day; owing to changes in literary convention translations, like accompaniments to folksongs, must sooner or later become out of date, and have to be rewritten.

English is a perfectly good language for singing, if singers will take the trouble to pronounce it naturally, as actors do. Even when English is difficult to sing, it is less difficult than German can be in some of the standard German operas. The first duty of a translator is to make the story of the opera clear, and to write words simple enough to be intelligible when sung. If only for this reason, the words must be accurately fitted to the music; and after all these conditions are fulfilled, there is not much chance left for 'poetry'. The reader is asked to remember that the words of these English versions have been written to be sung and acted, not to be read. Stage scenery is not meant to be hung in a private house; the scene-painter is satisfied if it looks reasonably well on the stage. If the reader discovers in these pages any line that he can call poetry, he may be sure that it has been stolen from some more respectable—and, I hope, non-copyright —author.

E. J. D.

Autumn, 1937

INTRODUCTION

DURING the Reign of Terror (1792–4), as the first two years of the first French Republic were called, Jean Nicolas Bouilly, a man of letters, engaged to be married to the daughter of the composer Grétry, held an administrative post in his native city, Tours, and thereby was a direct witness of many episodes of heroism and self-sacrifice on the part of his fellow citizens. In his spare time he was a writer of librettos for operas, and when the spirit of the Revolution led the musical public to desire realistic operas that reflected the feeling of the times, he utilized his own experiences for this purpose. He tells us in his autobiography (*Mes Récapitulations*, 1836) that the story of the opera *Léonore, ou l'amour conjugal* (*Leonora, or Wedded Love*), which was set to music by Pierre Gaveaux and performed in Paris in 1798, was perfectly true; the heroine was a lady of Tours whom he himself had helped to rescue her imprisoned husband. He transferred the episode to Spain and to the sixteenth century in order to avoid trouble with the authorities. Librettos in those days were regarded as common property, and Bouilly's *Léonore* was seized upon by two Italian composers, both now forgotten, but extremely popular in their day. Ferdinando Paër's setting was produced at Dresden in 1804 and a version in one act (the scene transferred to Poland) by Simone Mayr came out at Padua early in 1805.

Beethoven is often supposed to have had no understanding of the stage; but for the greater part of his life it was his keen desire to compose operas. The first work which made him famous in Vienna was the ballet

Prometheus (1801); in April 1803 he had a further success with the oratorio *The Mount of Olives*, which is almost more of an opera than an oratorio. Schikaneder, the director of the Theater an der Wien opened in 1801 and at that time considered to be the most magnificent theatre in Germany, wanted him to compose an opera; but although Beethoven went to live in rooms in the theatre, the plan did not take effect until after the theatre had been taken over by Baron von Braun in 1804. It was then decided that the opera should be based on Bouilly's *Léonore*, and Joseph Sonnleithner, secretary of the opera-house, was engaged to translate the book into German. The first performance, in November 1805, took place under unfortunate conditions. The French army under Bonaparte entered Vienna on 13 November and the Viennese nobility left the city; the opera was performed to an audience consisting mainly of French officers. After three performances Beethoven withdrew it. After drastic revisions it was performed again in March 1806.

There had been difficulties with the censorship over the first performance; in October 1805 Sonnleithner had had to write to the authorities begging that the refusal might be withdrawn. It is interesting to note that even at this date he calls the opera *Fidelio*. He suggests four reasons why the opera should be permitted: (1) because the Empress (Maria Theresa of Sicily) greatly admired the original libretto, (2) Paër's Italian *Leonora* had already been given at Dresden and Prague, (3) Beethoven had been at work on the score for a year and a half, and (4) good librettos were very scarce. The censorship seems to have objected to the story on political grounds. Sonnleithner points out that the plot was transferred to a remote country and to the sixteenth century; further, it treated only of a *private* revenge of the Governor Pizarro.

In 1814 Beethoven's opera was revised once again. The libretto was altered by Treitschke at Beethoven's request, and considerable changes were made in the music. On 23 May the opera was brought out in the form in which we now know it.

STORY OF THE OPERA

Florestan, a Spanish nobleman, has been thrown into prison by Pizarro, ostensibly for political reasons, but really on account of private enmity. All we are told in the opera is that Florestan got himself into trouble by speaking the truth too openly. His wife Leonora determines to rescue him; for this purpose she disguises herself as a man under the name of Fidelio and enters the service of Rocco, jailer of the prison. She wins the confidence of Rocco, but is embarrassed to find that Rocco's daughter Marcellina falls in love with the supposed young man, discarding her former lover, Jacquino, the porter. Pizarro, who is the Governor of the prison, is warned anonymously that Fernando, a Minister of State, intends to investigate the cases of prisoners in his charge; he therefore decides to have Florestan immediately put out of the way. As Rocco refuses to murder him, Pizarro undertakes to do so himself.

In Act II we see Florestan in his dungeon, almost crazy with suffering and exhaustion. Rocco and Leonora enter to dig a grave for him; not until this is finished does Leonora make sure that the man in the dungeon is her husband. He does not recognize her at all. Pizarro enters and reveals himself to Florestan; as he is about to murder him Leonora steps in and threatens him with a pistol.

At this moment a trumpet is heard; it is the signal to announce the arrival of the Minister. Pizarro is obliged to go and meet him, and Leonora is left alone with Florestan. The scene now changes to the outside of the prison. Don Fernando arrives, and is horrified to find his old friend Florestan in chains; he orders him to be set free at once and Pizarro to be handed over to justice. The opera ends with a chorus in praise of Leonora's heroic deed.

Bouilly's original libretto was in two acts, and Gaveaux's opera contained much less music than Beethoven's. Pizarro does not sing at all, except in ensembles. His instructions to Rocco are not sung, nor even spoken before the audience; the first act ends with a short chorus of prisoners coming out of their cells for exercise. In the dungeon scene the frustrated murder has no music except the sound of the trumpet. After Pizarro leaves the stage Leonora falls unconscious, and there is a pathetic duet in which Florestan struggles to comfort her but cannot reach her on account of his chain. A chorus is heard in the distance, which adds to their terror; they find, however, that it is the Minister with his train who comes to set Florestan free. There is no change to the open-air scene.

It is pretty certain that Beethoven must have seen the score of Gaveaux's opera; musically it is of no great value, but it shows a decided attempt to treat the subject in a serious and forceful style. It has been suggested that the story of the opera was told to Beethoven by Paër, who was in Vienna in 1803. There is also an anecdote to the effect that Beethoven heard Paër's setting in Paër's own company, and said to him (in French) that he would like to write music to that libretto himself. The words are sometimes quoted as an example of Beethoven's tactlessness; but in reality there would have been nothing offensive about them, as it was a common practice at that time, especially in Paris, for the same libretto to be set by several composers. The anecdote must, however, be dismissed as apocryphal, for there was no occasion on which the two composers could have been present at a performance of Paër's opera. Paër's music is much more attractive than Gaveaux's; it is rather Mozartian in style, and has some passages of deep feeling. It is most probable that Beethoven was acquainted with it.

Sonnleithner's main idea was to provide Beethoven with more opportunities for music than there had been in the French version. In doing this he rather lost sight of Bouilly's dramatic intentions. Rocco, in the French version, is a clearly defined character; the one thing about which he cares is money, and for money he will do anything. Sonnleithner either misunderstood this or thought it unpleasant; the result is that Rocco has no very decided personality at all. Another point that Sonnleithner modified was Marcellina's attachment to Fidelio; in the French version they sing a duet in which Marcellina talks about the children she hopes to bear him when they are married. In Paër's version Leonora has to have a love scene with Marcellina in the dungeon, in the presence of her own husband. In Mayr's the behaviour of Pizarro is explained by the fact that he cherishes a guilty passion for Leonora.

The two composers who most influenced Beethoven in *Fidelio* were Cherubini and Mozart. Cherubini's operas sound rather dry and old-fashioned now, but we ought to remember that they were wholeheartedly admired not only by Beethoven, but by Schubert, Weber, Mendelssohn, and Wagner. It was Cherubini and the other composers of the French Revolution, such as Gossec and

Lesueur, who first initiated that grave and loftily ethical style which we generally associate with the name of Beethoven. And *Fidelio* is also the natural sequel to *The Magic Flute*; Florestan and Leonora are Tamino and Pamina born again as real human beings, facing as realities what they had previously seen only as symbols.

LEONORA, OR WEDDED LOVE

Léonore, ou l'amour conjugal, words by J. N. Bouilly, music by Pierre Gaveaux, Paris, 1798.

Leonora, ossia l'amore coniugale, words adapted from Bouilly by G. Carpani, music by Ferdinando Paër, Vienna, 1804.

L'amor conjugale, 'farsa sentimentale' in one act, words adapted from J. N. Bouilly by Gaetano Rossi, music by Simone Mayr, Padua, early in 1805.

Fidelio, oder die eheliche Liebe, opera in three acts, words adapted from Bouilly by J. F. Sonnleithner, music by Beethoven, Vienna, 20 November 1805 (with the Overture now called 'Leonora No. 2').

Fidelio, oder die eheliche Liebe (second version), (*Fidelio* on the posters and programmes, but *Leonore* on the title-page of the libretto), in two acts, words from Bouilly by Sonnleithner, revised by Stephan von Breuning, music by Beethoven, Vienna, 29 March 1806 (with the Overture now called 'Leonora No. 3').

Fidelio, oder die eheliche Liebe (third version), opera in two acts, words adapted from Bouilly by J. F. Sonnleithner, revised by F. Treitschke, music by Beethoven, Vienna, 23 May 1814 (with the Overture now called 'Fidelio').

First performance in Paris, 5 May 1832.

First performance in London (in German), King's Theatre, 18 May 1832; (in English) Covent Garden, 12 June 1833.

First performance of this English version, Sadler's Wells Theatre, 3 November 1937.

CHARACTERS

(in the order of their appearance)

JACQUINO, porter at the prison	*Tenor*
MARCELLINA, daughter of Rocco	*Soprano*
ROCCO, jailer at the prison	*Bass*
LEONORA, wife of Florestan, disguised as a youth under the name of Fidelio	*Soprano*
PIZARRO, governor of the prison	*Bass*
FLORESTAN, a State prisoner, husband of Leonora	*Tenor*
FERNANDO, Minister of State	*Bass*
Chorus of Soldiers, Prisoners, and People	

Scene.—A State prison near Seville, in the sixteenth century.

ACT I

No. 1. Overture

SCENE 1. *The scene is the courtyard of a State prison. At the back is the main entrance, with a postern gate and a porter's lodge. On the left are heavily barred doors leading to the cells, with the jailer's house towards the foreground; on the right are trees, and a gate leading to a garden.*

  MARCELLINA *is ironing linen on a table outside her door, with a charcoal stove to heat her iron;* JACQUINO *is near the porter's lodge, and opens the gate for several people who bring in parcels, &c.*

[This is the original stage direction; but at some theatres the Act is divided into two scenes—the first ending after the Terzetto and being played in the interior of Rocco's house.]

No. 2. Duet

JAC. Come sweetheart, at last we're alone;
    I hope you've a moment to spare now.

MARC. (*continuing her work*).
    You'd much better wait till I've done,
     You can see I've got work to do—there now!

JAC. I've something to tell you, my dear.

MARC. Well, well, talk away, I can hear,
    But don't come too near.

JAC. You might be a little bit kinder,
    You won't let me utter a word.

MARC. I'd give you a gentle reminder,
    Your story too often I've heard.
    You're spoiling my work for the day!
     Talk on then for once in a way.

1

JAC. Be kind now and hear what I say,
      And then you may send me away.
      Well, I wanted—to ask you to marry me,
      You knew that?

MARC.   A long time ago.

JAC. Then, if you are willing to take me—
      And aren't you?

MARC.   To church we should go.

JAC. Our banns could be up then on Sunday.

MARC. So *you* think you've settled the day?
      Well done!

                                  Some one knocks.

JAC. Oh, plague on whoever is knocking!
      I thought I was just getting on,
      And now my chances are gone.

                        He goes to open the door.

MARC. Well, *that* business takes him away!
      I'm sorry that I led him on;
      I ought to have bid him begone.
      Poor boy, I can see how he suffers,
      I grieve that his heart is so sore;
      Fidelio my heart possesses,
      Fidelio alone I adore.

JAC. (*returning*).
      Where was I? I'll try her again.

MARC. Well, this time I'll have to be plain.

JAC. How long must I wait for your answer?
      Will you take me for weal or for woe?

MARC. (*aside*). There's nothing to do but refuse him.
      (*To him*). My answer, to-day and for ever, is 'No!'

JAC.   Your heart is as hard as a stone!

MARC. (*aside*). 'Tis painful to strike him a blow.
         (*To him.*) My answer will always be 'No'.

JAC.   Such cruelty why have you shown?

MARC. (*aside*). I must be as hard as a stone;
         How else his defeat will he own?

JAC.   Come—you don't think—
         Your mind you'll ever be changing?
         What think you?

MARC.   Get out of my way.

JAC.   What? I think you might
         At least just let me stop and look at you;
         Oh, mayn't I?

MARC.   Oh, well, you may stay.

JAC.   How often you faithfully promis'd—

MARC. I promis'd? Now you know
         I really never, never did;
         Such things you have no right to say.

JAC.   Yes, often you faithfully promis'd—

                            Knocking again.

         Oh, plague on whoever is knocking,
         Plague take them!
         She tells me I'm not to her taste;
           Why did she not say so before?
         With a refusal I am fac'd,
           However, I shall try my luck once more.

MARC. Well, *that* business takes him away!
         Quick open the door now, make haste,
           Run along, run and open the door!
         I tell you, I've no time to waste;
           So please don't say anything more.

JAC. Well, if I haven't opened that gate two hundred times this morning my name's not Jacquino! And I thought I was going to have a nice little chat with *you*! (*Knocking.*) Oh, the devil! There they are again!

                                                        Goes to open.

MARC. (*sighs*). I can't help it—but I don't seem to fancy Jacquino as much as I used to do.

JAC. (*at the door, to some one behind*). I'll see to it, that's right! (*Comes back to* MARCELLINA.) *Now* I hope we shan't be disturbed.

ROC. (*outside, calling*). Jacquino! Jacquino!

MARC. Father's calling you.

JAC. He can wait a moment. I want to tell you—

MARC. No, you *must* go; Father will want news of Fidelio.

JAC. Fidelio! He's always in such a state about Fidelio.

ROC. (*outside*). Jacquino! Where *are* you?

JAC. Coming, sir! (*To* MARCELLINA.) Now *you* stop here; I'll be back in a minute.

                                                        Exit.

MARC. Poor Jacquino! I'm really sorry for him. And the more I'm sorry for *him*, the more I understand how much I love Fidelio. And I think Fidelio loves me, too; so if we could once get father's consent, my happiness would be complete.

No. 3. ARIA

MARC.   Oh when shall I be bound to him
                  In wedlock fast united?
              My tongue is tied by modesty,
                  Before our troth is plighted.

How I desire his fond embrace,
I dare not to myself confess,
   Till naught can e'er divide us!
Let hope sustain my trembling heart,
Till I from him shall never part,
   And love to joy shall guide us.

How blest will be the humble cot,
   That I with him am sharing!
Contented we'll accept our lot,
   Each other's burdens bearing.

And when the work of day is done
His bosom I shall rest upon,
   For naught can e'er divide us.
May hope sustain my trembling heart,
Till I from him shall never part,
   And love to joy shall guide us.

Enter ROCCO.

ROC. Marcellina, has Fidelio not come back yet?

MARC. No, father.

ROC. But it's nearly time for me to take the dispatches to my lord the Governor, and Fidelio has not yet fetched them.

Knocking.

JAC. Coming! Coming!   *Runs across to open.*

MARC. Perhaps they kept him waiting at the blacksmith's.

Enter LEONORA.

Ah, there he is! there he is! (*Runs to help* LEONORA.) Poor Fidelio, you have indeed got a weight to carry.

LEON. I must admit, I am a little tired.

ROC. How much did it all cost?

LEON. About twelve piastres; here's the bill.

ROC. That's good; you're a clever lad to get things done so cheap. (*Aside.*) I suppose he's taking trouble to please Marcellina.

LEON. I did the best I could for you, sir.

ROC. (*significantly*). Well, you deserve your reward.

LEON. (*simply, not understanding*). Sir, 'twas only my duty.

ROC. Aha! do you think I cannot read your heart?

No. 4. QUARTET

MARC. (*aside*). My heart had told me so,
    Before one word he said.
He loves me, now I know;
    The path of joy I now may tread.

LEON. (*aside*). My heart is full of woe,
    And hope gives way to dread.
That child loves me, I know;
    Oh what a dangerous path I tread!

ROC. (*aside*). She loves the lad, I know,
    And well I wish them wed;
To church they soon shall go,
    And all my blessings on their head!

JAC. (*aside*). I can't think what to do,
    I must have lost my head.
How can she jilt me so,
    And take that lad instead?

ROC. Fidelio, I don't know who you are, or where you come from, but I'm going to make you my son-in-law.

MARC. (*excited*). How soon, father?

6

ROC. You're in a great hurry! You must wait till my lord the Governor goes to Seville; and then you can be married the next day.

MARC. The day after he goes; that's a very good idea.

LEON. (*with apparent delight*). The day after he goes! (*Aside.*) How shall I ever escape from this?

ROC. You seem to be very fond of one another! But remember, love's all very well, but it won't keep the pot boiling.

No. 5. ARIA

ROC. Love will not suffice for marriage,
　　You'll want love and something more;
　Or you'll find that life's a burden
　　When the wolf is at the door.

　But if you are sure of a balance in hand,
　　And always take thought for the morrow,
　You may not live on the fat of the land,
　　But you'll be protected from sorrow.

　So trust the wisdom of the old,
　And pin your faith to good red gold.

　Start your home without a penny,
　　You'll repent it very soon.
　Love upon an empty stomach
　　Plays a melancholy tune.

　But if you remember you must put away
　　A nice little hoard in your stocking,
　You'll prosper and flourish from day unto day,
　　Tho' children around you be flocking.

　Then trust the wisdom of the old,
　And pin your faith to good red gold.

7

LEON. There is something I value more than gold, sir, and that is *your confidence*; especially since I have so often seen you come back out of breath and exhausted after you have had to go down to the lower dungeons. Could not I help you with that work, sir?

ROC. You know I have the strictest orders never to allow any person, whoever it be, into the cells where the prisoners of State are shut up.

MARC. There are far too many of them here, father; you're working yourself to death.

LEON. Marcellina is quite right, sir; but I do indeed wish that I could do something to relieve you.
> *Takes* ROCCO'S *hand affectionately*.

MARC. You must consider your children, father!
> *Takes his other hand*.

ROC. You're quite right; it will be too much for me one of these days. My lord is very strict, but really he must allow me to take you with me into the secret dungeons. (LEONORA *makes a violent gesture of delight—then restrains herself*.) But there's one vault into which I shall never be able to take you, although I myself have entire confidence in you.

MARC. Where that prisoner is locked up—the one you told me about, father?

ROC. Yes.

LEON. He has been there a long time now, hasn't he?

ROC. Just over two years.

LEON. (*very excited*). Two years! (*Recovering herself*.) Then he must be a very dangerous criminal.

ROC. Or else have great enemies; it's much the same thing.

8

MARC. And nobody knows his name or who he is.

ROC. He would have told me all that himself, often enough.

LEON. But why not?

ROC. For the likes of us it's always best to know as few secrets as possible. (*Mysteriously.*) Anyway, he won't be troubling me much longer.

LEON. (*aside*). Oh, heavens!

MARC. Father dear, you had better not take Fidelio to see him; it would be too much for him to bear.

LEON. Do you doubt my courage?

ROC. That's right, my lad!

No. 6. Trio

ROC. Well said, my lad! and I am glad
    That you can face the duties of a prison,
Where, come what may, you must obey,
    Nor dare to ask a reason.

LEON. I know no fear, and I will bear
    Whatever terrors on my way befall me.
Love's prayer be heard, 'tis my reward;
    Not death, nor torture can appal me.

MARC. Your tender heart may feel distraught,
    At what you see before you;
Remember, love waits here above,
    With all delight to restore you.

ROC. Your fortune you will safely gather.

LEON. 'Twas Heaven's own hand that brought me hither.

MARC. How happy we shall be together,
    If you my love will not despise.

ALL.   For love has pow'r to win the prize.

ROC.   Now mark my words,
       I'll ask the Governor this morning
           To let you help me, if you may.

LEON.   I'm ready now if you should want me;
           Oh, let me come and help this day.

MARC.   Yes, father, ask him now, this morning,
           And then at once let us be wed!

ROC.   Yes, yes,
       I'll ask him now, this very morning,
           To let you help me, yes, this day.
       I fear that death has given me warning!
           I need your help, I do indeed.

LEON.   (*aside*).   How long have I in torment suffer'd!
           'Tis hope alone my way can lead.

MARC.   Why, dearest father, what did you say?
           You cannot leave us for many a day.

ROC.   I'll say no more, I must take care,
           For it is time that I was going.
       Take hand in hand, at love's command,
           While tears of joy are flowing.

MARC.   Take heart again, no more complain;
           What happiness I'm knowing!
       At love's command I take his hand,
           My heart with joy o'erflowing.

LEON.   I must refrain, I'll not complain,
           Nor grief of heart be showing;
       I give my hand and firm will stand,
           Tho' bitter tears be flowing.

SCENE 2. *The courtyard of the prison.*

No. 7. MARCH

Enter soldiers, and lastly PIZARRO. *Military business.*

PIZ. (*to the officer*). Three sentries on the wall; six men
   day and night on the drawbridge and another six in
   the garden. Whoever comes near the moat is to be
   brought before me at once. (*Enter* ROCCO.) Rocco,
   what news?

ROC. None, my lord.

PIZ. Where are the dispatches?

ROC. Here, my lord.

Gives dispatches.

PIZ. (*looks at them*). Whose writing is that? (*Reads.*)
   'An unknown friend warns you: Don Fernando, the
   Minister, has been informed that there are confined in
   your dungeons several victims of tyranny. He sets
   out to-morrow to visit the prison and take you by
   surprise. Be on your guard.' Ah! and suppose he finds
   Florestan imprisoned here—his dear friend Florestan,
   whom he believes to have died two years ago! (*Hesi-
   tating, then making up his mind.*) There is no other
   way; I must get rid of him at once.

No. 8. ARIA WITH CHORUS

PIZ.   Ha! Ha! Now is the moment come
              When I may wreak my vengeance.
              Yes, now Florestan shall die!
              Away with coward conscience!
              The mightier man am I;
              How nearly he once did make me
              The jest of those that hate me!

11

         How near he came
         In the dust to lay me low!
         Now is he in my power;
         Now strikes his fatal hour
         Who sought my overthrow.
         And as I stand before him,
         With deadly steel to gore him,
         I'll shout into his ear,
         'Tis I! 'Tis I! 'Tis I!
         'Tis I who triumph here!

SOLDIERS (*to each other*). His face is dark with anger,
         His looks portend some danger;
         There's grim work now before us here.
         Keep watch and ward:
         What comes may yet be stranger.

PIZ. Captain! (*The Captain comes forward and* PIZARRO *speaks to him in a low voice.*) Go up to the top of the tower; take a trumpeter with you. Keep the most careful look-out on the road to Seville. The moment you see a carriage with outriders coming this way, give a signal. You understand; the moment you see it in the distance, or your head shall answer for it. (*To the sentries.*) To your posts! Go! Rocco!

ROC. My lord?

PIZ. (*looks at him carefully for a moment—then, aside*). I must win him over; I can do nothing without his help. (*To* ROCCO.) Come here.

No. 9. DUET

PIZ.   Here, fellow, listen and take my order,
         You shall be well rewarded;
         Here (*gives money*), there'll be more to come.
         But make your mouth be dumb.

ROC. I wait, sir, on your order,
      What would you have me do?

PIZ. A man of nerve unshaken,
      Whom pity ne'er can weaken,
        Long service here has harden'd you.

ROC. What would you? Speak, sir, trust me!

PIZ. Murder!

ROC.   Sir!

PIZ. Listen, if you can;
      You quake, are you a man?
      Events are moving thickly;
        Before it be too late,
        A danger to the State
      Must be remov'd, and quickly.

ROC. Oh, sir!

PIZ. A danger to the State,
      Who's here a prisoner,
      He must be remov'd and quickly.
      Come, no delay,
      You must obey.
        (*Aside.*)
      So long as he is living,
        My power is not secure!
      How can I be forgiving?
        His death alone can make me sure.

ROC. I feel my limbs a-tremble,
        My conscience is secure;
      I will commit no murder,
        Whate'er I must endure.
      My lord, I am no hangman,
        'Tis not my duty to put a man to death.

PIZ.   Then I myself will kill him,
        If you daren't choke his breath.
      Make haste, and ask no reason;
      You know the man in prison——

ROC.   You mean that man
      That, like a ghost, scarce lives?

PIZ.   I do; go to his cell;
      I'll wait till all is ready.
      There us'd to be a well there;
      Quick, dig a grave.

ROC.   And then? and then?

PIZ.   I'll come, my face concealing,
      To his dungeon stealing;
      One blow, and that's the end.   *Shows his dagger.*

ROC.   In chains condemn'd to languish,
        He bore a life of pain.
      Death will but end his anguish
        And set him free again.

PIZ.   I'd rather see him languish
        In agony and pain;
      His death may end his anguish,
        It makes me safe again.

      Now, listen to what I tell you:
      When the grave is finish'd,
      You'll give a signal,
      And I my way will wend
      To where he lies in darkness;
      One blow, and that's the end.

      With joy I'd see him languish
        In agony and pain,

His death may end his anguish,
   But I am safe again.

ROC. In chains condemn'd to languish,
     He bore a life of pain.
    Death will but end his anguish
     And set him free again.

Exeunt PIZARRO *and* ROCCO *to garden.* LEONORA *has been watching on the stage during the duet; she now comes forward.*

No. 10. Recitative and Aria

LEON. Foul murderer!
    What brought you here? What would you do?
    Lives there a fiend in Hell so cruel?
    Can you not hear the voice of pity?
    No, no, 'tis only hate you feel.

Yet, though the tempest of your anger
   Harsher and ever harsher grows,
I see, beyond, a rainbow shining,
   That bright against the storm-cloud shows
And in my heart, so softly gleaming,
It speaks of love and grace redeeming.
   My fever'd blood now calmly flows.

Oh Hope, let not thy last faint star,
   In dark despair be blinded!
Fair light, point me the way afar,
   That love may safely find it.

I go, for love compels me,
   I know not fear,
   My path lies here,
My faithful heart now tells me.

15

> To him, my one and only one,
>> My course unfalt'ring presses;
> By hatred fast in fetters thrown,
>> He dreams of my caresses.
>> He waits till I release him.

                         Exit to garden.

Enter MARCELLINA, *followed at once by* JACQUINO.

JAC. But, Marcellina——

MARC. I won't hear another word of all this nonsense about love; you've had my answer once and for all.

JAC. Who'd have thought that, when I first fell in love with you? In those days it was always 'kind Jacquino, dear Jacquino' with you; but ever since Fidelio came here——

MARC. I did like you, I'll admit; but it wasn't really love. I never knew what that was until Fidelio——

JAC. Fidelio! Fidelio! Who's he, I should like to know? A young vagrant whom your father took in out of charity!

Enter ROCCO *and* LEONORA.

ROC. What are you two quarrelling about?

MARC. Jacquino's always wanting to marry me.

ROC. To marry you? (*Severely.*) Young man, you'll have to ask her father's consent first, and you won't get that in a hurry. I've got other matters to attend to.

MARC. I understand you, father; (*softly*) you mean Fidelio!
       LEONORA *is much embarrassed; then she tactfully changes the subject.*

LEON. Master Rocco, isn't to-day one of the days when the prisoners are allowed to walk in the garden?

MARC. Oh, yes, father, and such a glorious day too!

ROC. What, without my lord's permission?

LEON. He'll never know; he's busy with the dispatches. He won't be back for a long time.

MARC. He won't be too severe either; wasn't he asking you some sort of favour just now?

ROC. (*significantly*). A favour? He was indeed! Yes, I think we may risk it. Jacquino, Fidelio, take the keys and unlock the cells. I'll go and see my lord, (*to* MARCELLINA) and do my best for *you*.

MARC. Oh, thank you, father!

Kisses his hand.

Exit ROCCO. LEONORA *and* JACQUINO *unlock doors; the prisoners gradually come out.*

No. 11. FINALE

During the chorus LEONORA *looks intently at every prisoner in turn, hoping to discover her husband.*

PRISONERS. Oh, happy sight! How pure and bright
The air and light around us!
Here life again has found us;
Our prison is a grave.

A PRISONER. The mercy everlasting of God
Will comfort all who trust Him.
There speaks the voice of hope in me,
God's help is nigh, and we may yet go free.

PRISONERS. Oh, freedom, freedom! Heavenly powers!
Oh, freedom! Will it yet be ours?

ANOTHER   Be silent, never speak that word;
PRISONER.   Here we are watch'd and overheard.

17

PRISONERS. Remember, one forbidden word
On our lips never may be heard.

The prisoners, directed by JACQUINO *and* MARCEL-
LINA, *move towards the garden.*

Enter ROCCO.

LEON. Now what's the news?

ROC. My promise stands;
I took my courage in my hands,
And told him who you were, and what you
wanted.
And you shall hear what he said.
Your wedding, my fine son-in-law,
He gladly granted; and I may take you
To help me in the dungeon down below.

LEON. To the dungeon, the dungeon!
Oh, happy day, my prayer is granted!

ROC. Your help will soon be wanted,
But yet a little while,
And we'll go down together,
Down to work we'll go together.

LEON. Go down?

ROC. To darkness far below,
Where lies a prisoner fetter'd,
And dying of starvation slow.

LEON. Ha! May we now release him?
What then?

ROC. No, no, 'twill not be so.
Release him—yes—but how?
Before this hour is ended
(I have a secret order),
The grave will bring him peace.

18

LEON.	Then he is dead?
ROC.	Not yet.
LEON.	Are you to murder him yourself?
ROC.	No, I will not that duty bear; Of murder I keep my conscience clear. 'Twill be my lord Pizarro strikes the fatal blow; We only dig the grave below.
LEON.	And in that grave my husband bury! With what torment I'm oppress'd!
ROC.	Of slow starvation he is dying; God grant his soul eternal rest! We dare not stay a moment longer; I want your help, your arms are stronger. Such work is a jailer's daily bread.
LEON.	I'll follow you, were 't unto death.
ROC.	The ruin'd well we must re-open— An easy task for you and me, Yet gruesome, and I fain would spare you; For your young eyes 'tis hard to see.
LEON.	To one so young as I, 'Tis fearful to see a man die.
ROC.	I would have spar'd you this indeed, But I am old; your help I need. Besides, my lord must be obey'd.
LEON.	Oh, help me, heaven!
ROC.	(*aside*). The lad is weeping. (*Aloud.*) No, you stay here, I shall be able To do the work without your aid.

LEON.	No, let me come, I must indeed,
	I must indeed, whatever happens;
	That wretched man, I mean to see him,
	Tho' I should die myself with him.
ROC.	No, you stay here, I'll go alone.
BOTH.	We dare no longer now delay;
	Stern duty calls, we must obey.

Enter MARCELLINA *and* JACQUINO.

MARC.	Oh, father, come at once!
ROC.	What is it now?
JAC.	You're wanted here!
ROC.	What can it be?
MARC. ⎱	My lord Pizarro's in a rage;
JAC. ⎰	He's coming to look for you.
ROC.	Then let him come.
LEON.	We must away!
ROC.	Jacquino, say, does he know?
JAC.	Yes, indeed he does.
MARC.	He's in a rage, since you let
	The prisoners out for recreation.
ROC.	Then take them back again to prison.
MARC.	I dread Pizarro's anger,
	When he's in such a mood.
LEON.	This moment's full of danger,
	There's fever in my blood.
ROC.	I know I acted rightly,
	He should have understood.

Enter PIZARRO.

PIZ.   How dare you venture, on your own sole right,
       To allow the prisoners out?
       What right have you to give permission?
       You shall be punish'd for this crime.

ROC.   (*seeking for an excuse*). My lord!

PIZ.   Come, speak the truth.

ROC.   'Tis a fine spring morning—
       The sun is shining bright and warm—
       And—   *More composed.*
       And your lordship must remember,
       There's yet a better reason too;
       Our sovereign lord the King, God bless him!
       This is the day when he was born,
       And thus 'tis kept.

                                   Secretly to PIZARRO.

       Down there comes death—
       So may not these above
       Still enjoy their day of gladness?
       That man awaits your deadly blow.

PIZ.   Go dig the grave, make haste, be ready;
       Here I will wait, with none to watch me.
       Quick, put them under lock and key;
       Never dare tell what you may see,
       Tell not a soul what you may see.

The prisoners are driven back to their cells.

PRISONERS. Farewell to spring and morning ray,
                 Too brief a radiance lending,
            Farewell! we wend our dreary way,
                 Back to our shades descending,
                 Where chill dread waits unending,
            And time brings night, but no more day.

MARC.   (*looking at the prisoners*).
             They hail'd the spring, the morning ray;
                 Now their brief joy is ending.
                 Their dreary way they're wending.
             They bid farewell to happy day,
                 Back to their shades descending.

LEON. }   (*to the prisoners*).
JAC.   }   You hail'd the spring, the morning ray;
                 Now your brief joy is ending.
                 Your dreary way be wending;
             So bid farewell to happy day,
                 Back to your shades descending.

MARC.   For mercy on prisoners and captives
             With fervent heart I now should pray;
             For mine alone has joy to-day,
                 While they in tears and grief are sighing.
             They saw the light, and bless'd its ray;
                 Now hope for them is dying.

LEON.   Is there on earth no justice?
             Or is the tyrant free to slay?
             They saw the light and bless'd its ray;
                 Now hope for them is dying.

JAC.   (*aside, watching* ROCCO *and* LEONORA).
             Some plot I think they're hatching,
                 But I can't hear one word they say.
             With jealousy I'm raging;
                 But she'll repent it one fine day.

PIZ.   No more: go, my command obey.

ROC.   I will, my lord, without delay.

PIZ.   Go down into the dungeon.

ROC.   I'll go, my lord, without delay.
(*aside*). I dare not disobey him,
Dreadful the task before me!
    But yet I dare not disobey,
All must be done in secret,
    The time is short, I'll not delay.

PIZ.   The time is short, make no delay,
And think not of returning
    Till in his grave that man you lay.
All must be done in secret.
Go down you must, and that at once,
Go down into the dungeon.

Yes, now at last I'll have revenge,
    The one desire I cherish;
He no more shall thwart my will,
    And I this day shall see him perish.

END OF ACT I

ACT II

SCENE 1. *A dungeon. At the back is a wall with large irregular openings, made secure by gratings, through which a flight of steps can be seen, leading to a door in the wall. In front, at one side is a low entrance to a dark cell; on the other side, a mass of ruins and stones. The whole scene presents a ruinous appearance.*

FLORESTAN *is sitting on a stone; he is chained to the wall by a long chain fastened round his body.*

No. 12. RECITATIVE AND ARIA

FLOR. God! This awful dark!
How horrible the silence!
Here in my lonely cell
Ne'er a living thing I see.
Oh cruel fortune!
Yet the will of God is righteous;
I'll not complain, for all my sufferings come from
    Him.

Ere my life is half completed,
    All that gave me joy is flown;
Words of truth too boldly spoken,
    Brought me here to die alone.

All my pain I gladly suffer,
    End my life without a moan.
This alone consoles my sorrow,
    That my duty I have done.

(*Calm, but as though in an ecstasy.*)
Who is it, that figure so radiant and bright,
    That vision arising before me?

24

An angel in garment of light,
  With soft word of comfort and love to restore
  me!

My angel Leonora, my angel, my wife,
Yes, whom God sends to lead me to heavenly life!

I see her, I see her in glory so bright,
An angel, an angel in garment of light,
  I hear her with soft word of comfort restore me,
She leads me to freedom and heavenly life,
Yes, my Leonora, my angel, my wife!

*He sinks down exhausted and lies so that his face is
not visible either to the audience or to persons on the
stage.*

ROCCO *comes down the stairs at the back, followed
by* LEONORA; *he carries a lantern and a bottle of
wine.* LEONORA *carries a pickaxe and a spade.*

No. 13. MELODRAMA AND DUET

LEON. How cold it is in this underground vault!

ROC. Of course it is; it's a long way down.

LEON. (*looking anxiously round in every direction*). I
thought we should never find the entrance.

ROC. There's the man.

LEON. He seems not to move at all.

ROC. Perhaps he is dead.

LEON. You think so?

ROC. No, no, he is only asleep. All to the good. We
must get to work at once; we have no time to lose.

LEON. (*aside*). It is so dark, I cannot distinguish his
features. Oh, God help me, if it is my husband!

ROC. Somewhere underneath this rubbish is the old well.
  We shall not have to dig far to clear the opening.
  Give me the pickaxe. You stand there and shovel the
  stuff away. You're shivering? Are you frightened?

LEON. No, no, I'm only so cold.

ROC. Well then, set to work; that'll soon make you warm.
  *ROCCO begins to work; LEONORA tries to look at the
  prisoner while ROCCO is stooping.*

DUET

ROC. Come, set to work, for time is pressing;
  We have not long to dig the grave.

LEON. With all my strength I'm here to help you,
  No fault to find with me you'll have.

ROC. (*lifting a great stone*).
  Then come, stand by and help me lift the stone up;
  Take care and hold it fast.

LEON. (*helps to lift it*).
  I'm holding it—push below—
  I'll do the best I can to move it.

ROC. 'Tis nearly out.

LEON. Take care!

ROC. It moves.

LEON. Come, lift again!

ROC. A pretty weight!

LEON. We have it now——
  They let the stone roll down.

ROC. Come, set to work, my lord is waiting,
  And very soon he will appear.

LEON. A moment's rest, and I am ready,
There's not much more remains to clear.
Aside, trying to look at the prisoner.
That man, whoe'er he be, I'll save him!
I swear, I will not let him die;
Yes, 'tis I will save his life.

ROC. Come, come, get back to work, make haste!

LEON. (*begins to dig*).
I'm here, I'll help you, not a moment let me waste.

ROC. Be quick, I want your hand, set to!

LEON. There is not much for us to do.

ROC. Come, set to work, for time is pressing.

LEON. With all my strength I'm here to help you.

ROC. We have not long to dig the grave.

LEON. A moment's rest, and I am ready;
For soon Pizarro will appear.

BOTH. The hideous task at length is over;
The dead man's grave stands open here.

ROCCO *drinks from his bottle, while* LEONORA *looks intently at* FLORESTAN.

LEON. He's awake!

ROC. (*stops drinking*). Awake? Then he'll have a hundred questions to ask me. I must talk to him alone. (*Comes up out of the grave.*) You go down there and clear away.

Leonora goes into the grave.

(*To* FLORESTAN, *kindly.*) Well, sir, have you had a rest?

FLOR. Rest! Where can I ever find rest?

LEON. (*aside*). That voice! If I could only see his face—

FLOR. Hard-hearted man! are you always deaf to my complaints?

He turns towards LEONORA.

LEON. My husband!

Falls senseless on edge of grave.

ROC. What do you want? I have to carry out my orders.

FLOR. Tell me, who is the Governor of this prison?

ROC. (*aside*). There can be no harm in telling him that now. (*To* FLORESTAN.) The Governor of this prison is Don Pizarro.

LEONORA is recovering.

FLOR. Then for mercy's sake send a message to Seville, to my wife, Leonora Florestan.

LEON. (*aside*). She digs his grave.

FLOR. Tell her that I am here in chains——

ROC. 'Tis impossible, I say; it would be *my* ruin, and do *you* no good.

FLOR. If I am condemned to die in this dungeon, let me at least die quickly.

LEON. (*aside*). Oh, this passes endurance!

FLOR. For pity's sake let me have a drop of water.

ROC. I can't give you that; but there's just a drop of wine in the bottle you can have.

LEON. (*bringing bottle*). Here it is.

FLOR. Who is that?

ROC. My new helpmate. (*Genially.*) He's going to marry my daughter. Not much wine left, but you're very welcome to it. (*To* LEONORA.) What's the matter?

28

LEON. (*softly to* ROCCO, *with suppressed emotion*). You seem moved yourself, sir.

ROC. I can't help it; he has a voice——

LEON. A voice that rends my heart!

No. 14. TRIO

FLOR.   Be your good deed in Heav'n recorded,
      For surely 'twas Heav'n sent you here,
      My last remaining hour to cheer,
  Although with thanks alone by me rewarded.

ROC.   Poor soul, the wine I gladly give;
  Few moments more he has to live.

LEON.   My heart beats loud within my breast,
  With joy, and yet with fear and pain opprest.
  For now must I, his faithful wife,
  Face death myself, or save his life.

FLOR.   How strangely mov'd the lad appears!
  And ev'n the man seems half in tears.
  And hope again revives in me,
  That I may yet find liberty.

ROC.   I have my duty here to do,
  But hate the deed no less than you.

LEON. (*taking a piece of bread from her pocket*).
      This piece of bread may I not give him?
      He makes my heart with pity bleed.

ROC.   A kindly thought that is indeed,
  But yet I know I must forbid it.

LEON. (*ingratiatingly*).
      Yet you the wine yourself did give.
      Few moments more he has to live.

ROC. I have my orders to fulfil;
     I must obey my master's will.
     Then give it, yes, you may,
     I'll not refuse you.

LEON. (*greatly moved, offers bread to* FLORESTAN).
      Oh, take and eat this bread,
      Unhappy man!

FLOR. Oh, take my grateful thanks!
      'Tis more than I can e'er repay.

LEON. Oh, place your trust in Heaven above,
           You know not yet how near its help may be.
      (*To* ROCCO.)
      Your kindly help you too did give.
      Poor hapless man!
           'Tis more than I can bear to see.

ROC. Your sufferings fill'd my heart with pain,
          Although to help I was not free.
     Poor soul, my help I gladly give;
     Few moments more he has to live.
     Unhappy man!
          'Tis more than I can bear to see.

After the trio there is a moment's silence. Then
ROCCO *takes* LEONORA *aside.*

ROC. I must give my lord the signal.

Goes to back.

FLOR. Where is he going? (ROCCO *at back blows a whistle.*)
      Is that my death-knell?

LEON. No, no—dear friend—be calm——

FLOR. (*hysterical*). Oh, my Leonora! Shall I never see
      you again?

30

LEON. (*makes a great effort to control herself*). Be calm,
   I tell you. Whatever you may hear or see, never for-
   get that Providence watches over you.

                              She moves towards the grave.

                         Enter PIZARRO.

PIZ. (*in a muffled voice*). Is everything ready?

ROC. Yes; we have only the well to open.

PIZ. Send the lad away.

ROC. (*to* LEONORA). You must go.

LEON. And you?

ROC. I must stop to unlock the fetters. Go, go.

         LEONORA *retires to a dark part of the stage.*

PIZ. (*aside*). I must get rid of *both* these two to-day;
   then *everything* will be buried in that grave.

ROC. Shall I take off his irons, my lord?

PIZ. No.

                              Draws a dagger.

                   NO. 15. QUARTET

PIZ.   So die then! Yet, before you perish,
             I'd have you know who strikes the blow.
         No more I'll hide my secret vengeance;
             My name you, ere you die, shall know.
                         Throwing back his cloak.
         Pizarro! Did you seek my ruin?
         Pizarro! 'Twas your own undoing!
         Pizarro stands here to wreak his vengeance now.
         No longer need I now dissemble!
         Come, look upon my face and tremble!
         I stand before you here,
         To wreak my vengeance now.

                              31

FLOR.   (*calmly*). So murder, not justice, is your end?

PIZ.   'Twas you alone who sought my overthrow,
        One moment more is all you have to live.

        He attempts to stab FLORESTAN; LEONORA *rushes
        forward and covers* FLORESTAN *with her body.*

LEON.   No, no, you shall not, while I stand by his side,
        You shall not wreak your vengeance,
        Till I for him have died.

FLOR.   O God!

ROC.   How now? (*Hurls her away.*) What would you
            dare?
        Yes, you shall die for this.

FLOR.   O God!

PIZ.   Stand back! Would you dare?

LEON.   (*again protecting her husband*).
        I am his wife.

PIZ. }
ROC. } His wife?

FLOR.   My wife!

LEON.   (*to* FLORESTAN). Yes, I am Leonora!

FLOR.   Leonora!

LEON.   (*to the others*).
        I am his wife, and will not let him die,
        Spite all your power!

PIZ.   Would she my power defy?

FLOR.   My heart stands still for joy.

ROC.   My heart stands still for fear.

PIZ.   Shall I before a woman tremble?
            Another victim I will have.

Since you have shar'd his life and fortune,
His death as well you now may share.

LEON. I swear you shall not wreak your vengeance
While I stand by his side.
Move but a step, I shoot you dead!

*PIZARRO presses towards FLORESTAN; LEONORA
presents a pistol at him. A trumpet signal is heard.*

LEON. (*embracing FLORESTAN*).
Ah! You are deliver'd! Thanks to God!

FLOR. Ah! I am deliver'd! Thanks to God!

PIZ. (*stunned*). Ha! That was the signal! All is lost!

ROC. (*stunned*). Oh! What is that sound? Thanks be to
God!

> *The trumpet sounds again, nearer.*

*After the second trumpet signal JACQUINO appears
at the top of the staircase, with men carrying torches.
The torch-bearers remain at the top, whilst JAC-
QUINO hurries down towards ROCCO, but does not
come to the front, or even as far as the bottom of the
stairs.*

JAC. Master Rocco! The Minister is coming here; his
outriders are already at the gates.

ROC. (*aside*). Thanks be to God! (*To JACQUINO, very
loud.*) We'll come at once. Let those men with torches
come down and light the way up for my lord the
Governor.

> *The torch-bearers come down towards the front of
> the stage, so that during the rest of the music
> PIZARRO is fully illuminated by them, and conceal-
> ment is impossible.*

LEON.   Now strikes the hour of vengeance;
              Your dangers all are past.
         Through courage and devotion
              I'll set you free at last.

FLOR.   Now strikes the hour of vengeance;
              My dangers all are past.
         Your courage and devotion
              Will set me free at last.

PIZ.   Accurst who thwarts my vengeance!
              Not yet my hour is past.
         Despairing frenzy fills me;
              I'll have revenge at last.

ROC.   Now strikes the hour of vengeance;
              Are all his dangers past?
         Her courage and devotion
              May set him free at last.

The torch-bearers escort PIZARRO *upstairs.* ROCCO
follows with JACQUINO. LEONORA *and* FLORESTAN
are left alone.

FLOR.   Leonora!

LEON.   Florestan!

No. 16. Duet

LEON.⎫   Oh, joy beyond expressing,
FLOR.⎭   When heart finds heart again!
         Our anguish all forgotten
              In love's exultant strain!

LEON.   Once more within my arms I fold you.

FLOR.   By God's great mercy I behold you.

FLOR.⎫   Oh, thank we God whose tender care
LEON.⎭   Has given us now this joy to share.

34

    My life! My love!
    Oh joy beyond expressing!
    My love! My life!

FLOR. Leonora!

LEON. Florestan!

           Scene closes.

    SCENE 2. *Outside the prison.*

     No. 17. FINALE

CHORUS OF ⎫ Hail, happy day, day of rejoicing!
PEOPLE AND ⎬ So long desir'd, so long denied,
PRISONERS. ⎭ When Justice comes, with Mercy joining,
      The prison gates to open wide.

  Enter FERNANDO *and* PIZARRO, *escorted by soldiers.*

FERN.   Our sovereign lord the King commands me
      To succour all who suffer here;
     He for your wrongs has retribution,
      Long tho' you pin'd in gloom and fear.
     No longer kneel like slaves before me;
      No cruel tyrant is your king.
     To him his subjects are his brothers;
      To all he loves his help to bring.

  ROCCO *pushes through the guards accompanied by*
  LEONORA *and* FLORESTAN.

ROC.   Then here is one who needs his mercy!

PIZ.   My victim! No! Away!

ROC.   You're mov'd at last!

FERN. Speak on, then.

ROC.   God Almighty
     Has rais'd him from the dead again,
     Don Florestan—

       35

FERN. (*astonished*).   Yes, dead I thought him,
        That noble soul, for truth who fought—

ROC.   And on himself thus anguish brought.

FERN.   Belovèd friend, long dead I thought him!
        In fetters, pallid, he draws near.

LEON. }
ROC.   }   Yes, Florestan himself stands here.

ROC.   And Leonora.

                         Presenting her.

FERN. (*still more astonished*). Leonora?

ROC.   That noble lady 'tis indeed,
        She came to me—

PIZ.   A word with you, sir—

FERN.   No more!—she came?—

ROC.   —Here in her need,
        And, as a boy disguis'd, she serv'd me,
        Serv'd me so truly that my daughter
        At last to wed this youth agreed.

MARC.   Oh, father, what has fate decreed?

ROC.   That wretch there at this very moment
        Was waiting Florestan to slay.

PIZ.   'Twas he, he too!

ROC.   He would have kill'd him,
        But your arrival his hand did stay.

CHORUS.   Let justice on the assassin fall
        For cruelty so base!
        Let justice draw her flaming sword,
        The righteous to release!

             PIZARRO *is taken away by soldiers.*

FERN.	You did the prisoner's grave prepare;
	   Now loose his chains, and set him free.
	No, stay—lady, 'tis yours alone
	   Thus to complete his liberty.

LEON.	Oh, Heaven, can I believe my sight?
FLOR.	Oh, wond'rous hour of pure delight!
FERN.	'Tis God alone defends the right.
MARC. ROC.	And sends us after darkness light. *Chorus repeat.*

CHORUS.	Happy he whom Heav'n has granted
	   To be lov'd by such a wife!
	Praise we now the noble lady,
	   Saviour of her husband's life!

FLOR.	Your brave heart from death preserv'd me, Ended all my torment here.

LEON.	Love it was that gave me courage,
	   Steadfast love that knows no fear.
	
	Love it was that gave me courage,
	   To endure that bitter strife.
	Greater joy could none be granted,
	   Florestan returns to life.

CHORUS.	Come, let us all our voices raise, Loud in Leonora's praise.
FLOR. ROC. MARC. JAC. FERN. CHORUS.	Happy he whom Heav'n has granted To be lov'd by such a wife! Praise we now the noble lady, Saviour of her husband's life!

THE END

37

SET IN
GREAT BRITAIN
AT THE
UNIVERSITY PRESS
OXFORD
AND REPRINTED
PHOTOGRAPHICALLY
BY
GROSVENOR PRESS
PORTSMOUTH